PROTEST MOVEMENTS

CIVIL RIGHTS
SIT-INS

BY DUCHESS HARRIS, JD, PHD

Core Library

Cover image: Civil rights activists hold a sit-in in
Charlotte, North Carolina.

An Imprint of Abdo Publishing
abdopublishing.com

abdopublishing.com

Published by Abdo Publishing, a division of ABDO, PO Box 398166, Minneapolis, Minnesota 55439. Copyright © 2018 by Abdo Consulting Group, Inc. International copyrights reserved in all countries. No part of this book may be reproduced in any form without written permission from the publisher. Core Library™ is a trademark and logo of Abdo Publishing.

Printed in the United States of America, North Mankato, Minnesota
092017
012018

Cover Photo: Bruce Roberts/Science Source
Interior Photos: Bruce Roberts/Science Source, 1, 26–27; Atlanta Journal-Constitution/AP Images, 4–5; Russell Lee/FSA/OWI Collection/Library of Congress, 7; Bettmann/Getty Images, 12–13; AP Images, 17, 34–35; FK/AP Images, 18; Science Source, 20–21; Everett Collection/Newscom, 24; Red Line Editorial, 29, 40; The Herald in Rock Hill/AP Images, 31; Michael Ochs Archives/Getty Images, 38–39

Editor: Marie Pearson
Imprint Designer: Maggie Villaume
Series Design Direction: Claire Mathiowetz
Contributor: Rebecca Rowell

Publisher's Cataloging-in-Publication Data

Names: Harris, Duchess, author.
Title: Civil rights sit-ins / by Duchess Harris.
Description: Minneapolis, Minnesota : Abdo Publishing, 2018. | Series: Protest movements | Includes online resources and index.
Identifiers: LCCN 2017947138 | ISBN 9781532113963 (lib.bdg.) | ISBN 9781532152849 (ebook)
Subjects: LCSH: Civil rights demonstrations--Juvenile literature. | Civil rights movements--United States--History--20th century--Juvenile literature. | United States--Race relations--Juvenile literature. | Protest movements--Juvenile literature.
Classification: DDC 323.1196073--dc23
LC record available at https://lccn.loc.gov/2017947138

CONTENTS

BREAKING BARRIERS AT WOOLWORTH

On February 1, 1960, four college students sat down at the Woolworth store lunch counter in Greensboro, North Carolina, and ordered coffee. David Richmond, Franklin McCain, Ezell Blair Jr., and Joseph McNeil were African Americans. The store's lunch counter was for white people only.

The store wouldn't serve the four young men. The four knew that would happen. But they refused to move. They would not leave. They would sit as a way of taking

The Woolworth lunch counter, where people could sit on stools and order lunch, refused to serve African Americans.

a stand for civil rights. They became known as the Greensboro Four.

FIGHTING FOR EQUALITY

White people had treated African Americans as inferior for hundreds of years. Some white people who kept them enslaved until the 1860s considered them property. The end of slavery didn't end the unequal treatment of African Americans in the United States. Whites enforced segregation, passed race-based laws, and used violence against African Americans.

In the South, a variety of laws segregated the races. African Americans were kept separate from white people in public places such as buses, libraries, and restaurants. They had to use separate bathrooms and attend separate schools.

African Americans were tired of the unfair and unequal treatment. Some began fighting for equal rights. They included four students attending North

Signs noting "Whites Only" or "Colored" indicated which customers a business served.

Carolina Agricultural and Technical State University (NCATSU).

CAREFULLY PLANNED

Blair, McCain, McNeil, and Richmond often discussed racial inequality at NCATSU. A violent incident in 1955 stood out for them. That year, two white men in Mississippi tortured and killed Emmett Till. The 14-year-old African-American youth had supposedly flirted with a white woman. Despite evidence to the

In 1963, African-American author Anne Moody took part in a sit-in at the Jackson, Mississippi, Woolworth's lunch counter. An angry mob poured food on the protesters' heads and assaulted them. One dragged Moody by her hair to the store's door. She got up and returned to the counter. Moody wrote later, "After the sit-in, all I could think of was how sick Mississippi whites were. . . . Before the sit-in, I had always hated the whites in Mississippi. Now I knew it was impossible for me to hate sickness. The whites had a disease, an incurable disease in its final stage."

contrary, a jury of white men found Till's killers innocent. The four students decided they would do something to declare their stance against this and other injustices.

At 4:30 p.m. on February 1, 1960, the four college students entered the Woolworth store. They bought a few small items. Next, they went to the lunch counter. They sat down. The manager told the worker behind the counter to ignore the four men. He hoped they would simply leave. They did not. They stayed until the store closed at 5:30 p.m. They risked verbal and physical attacks by angry whites, but neither happened that afternoon. However, both soon would.

SPARKING A MOVEMENT

This sit-in protest launched a movement. The Woolworth lunch counter sit-in continued and grew. Blair, McCain, McNeil, and Richmond returned to the lunch counter and sat peacefully again on February 2. More than a dozen other students from NCATSU joined them.

On the third day, even more students took part in the sit-in. They took most of the lunch counter's 65 seats. Some protesters held a sit-in at the neighboring department store. Three white female college students joined the protest on the fourth day. By the fifth day, the number of students taking part had grown to 300. That day the police made their first arrests. They arrested three white men for intimidating protesters. One of the men had set a black protester's coat ablaze.

INTERNATIONAL CIVIL RIGHTS MUSEUM

The Woolworth sign is still visible in downtown Greensboro. But the building is no longer a drug store. The site is home to the International Civil Rights Center and Museum. The museum's exhibits include the lunch counter where Blair, McCain, McNeil, and Richmond held their sit-in protest in 1960.

But the abuse continued. White men and teenagers verbally attacked the sit-in participants. And as more people joined the civil rights cause, the number of people resisting grew as well.

National news coverage helped the cause. In a matter of weeks, the civil rights sit-in movement grew to include 55 cities in 13 states. That summer Woolworth ended its whites-only policy. The simple but powerful and brave action taken by four African-American college students had made a difference. They set into motion the civil rights sit-in movement. Sit-ins did much more than help integrate public facilities. They helped the civil rights movement progress.

STRAIGHT TO THE
SOURCE

When Franklin McCain died in 2014, civil rights activist and Georgia politician John Lewis spoke about him:

> Franklin McCain must be looked upon as one of the founding fathers of the sit-in movement. He was one of the four students who inspired an entire generation of young men and women, black and white, to stand-up by sitting down. Dr. Martin Luther King Jr. said that the four young men who sat down in Greensboro taught us all how to use the power of passive resistance on a mass scale. . . .
>
> Every citizen of this country owes him a debt of gratitude because he insisted that we create a more fair, more just democracy. We are a better people and a better country because Franklin McCain lived.
>
> Source: "Rep. Lewis Mourns the Loss of Greensboro Protestor Franklin McCain." *John Lewis*. US House of Representatives, January 10, 2014. Web. Accessed June 11, 2017.

Back It Up

What is one of the points Lewis is making? Write a paragraph describing this point. Include two or three pieces of evidence he uses to support this point.

SEPARATE AND UNEQUAL

The inequality Blair, McCain, McNeil, and Richmond were protesting had existed for a long time. It began with slavery even before the United States was a nation. The first people from Africa arrived in the colonies in 1619. A Dutch ship delivered the 20 Africans to Jamestown, Virginia. Colonists in Virginia needed people to help with farming. They enslaved Africans to work the farms. It was cheaper than hiring workers. Slavery continued throughout the 1700s and into the 1800s. Most slaves were on the southern coast.

An artist depicts a Dutch ship bringing enslaved people to Jamestown.

13

ABOLITIONISTS

Abolitionists were people who worked to end slavery in the United States. Some were white, and some were African American. White people tended to focus only on ending slavery. But African Americans also focused on gaining equal rights. Sojourner Truth was an abolitionist who escaped from slavery in 1827. In an 1851 speech, she responded to the common practice of white men helping white women: "Nobody ever helps me into carriages, or over mud-puddles, or gives me any best place! And ain't I a woman?"

Slavery divided the nation. It led to the American Civil War (1861–1865). The Southern states, known as the Confederacy, wanted to leave the United States and keep slavery. The Northern states, known as the Union, wanted to keep the nation together. On January 1, 1863, President Abraham Lincoln released the Emancipation Proclamation. In it, he declared all slaves in the Confederacy free. After the war, the 13th Amendment officially abolished slavery. It was added to the Constitution on December 18, 1865.

JIM CROW

The Civil War freed approximately 3 million slaves. But the end of slavery did not end whites' mistreatment of blacks. For many years after the war, southern states created laws that segregated blacks and whites. These became known as Jim Crow laws. Jim Crow was a negative name for African Americans. Jim Crow laws separated African Americans from white people in most areas of life.

SEPARATE BUT EQUAL

In 1896 the US Supreme Court ruled on *Plessy v. Ferguson*. The case was about segregated train cars. Homer Plessy was arrested on June 7, 1892, for sitting in a seat designated for white people only. Plessy was African American. The Court ruled against Plessy. The ruling stated that separate accommodations were fine if they were of equal quality and didn't go against the US Constitution. With this ruling, the US Supreme Court said segregation was okay.

BROWN V. BOARD OF EDUCATION

The separate facilities were supposed to be of equal quality. But those for African Americans often were not as good as those made available to white people. This included schools. White students usually had clean classrooms. Textbooks and other materials were new. Black students attended schools that were falling apart. Their books were used. Some schools did not have a lunchroom. Sometimes there were too many kids for the school to hold. One school used school buses as classrooms.

In the early 1950s, some African Americans sued their states over the poor quality of schools. Lawyers argued before state courts that African American students did not have access to the same quality of education as white students. Segregated schools were the cause of this. Judges ruled against all five cases. The lawyers asked the US Supreme Court to hear the cases. It heard them as a single case. The case was called *Brown v. Board of Education*.

George E. C. Hayes, *left*, Thurgood Marshall, *middle*, and James M. Nabrit were lawyers who fought segregation in *Brown v. Board of Education*.

On May 17, 1954, all nine justices made the same decision. They said separate but equal policies did not work in schools. The ruling made school segregation illegal.

Soldiers continued to guard the Little Rock Nine throughout the school year.

LITTLE ROCK NINE, 1957

While the Supreme Court had made school segregation illegal, desegregation faced much opposition. In 1957, nine African-American students in Little Rock, Arkansas, enrolled in the all-white Little Rock Central High School. School authorities told the students not to show up on the first day of school. They didn't. But they did attend the second day. A mob of white people threw rocks and yelled at them. Some people said they would kill the teenagers. The students also faced approximately 100 soldiers from the state's National Guard, whom the governor of Arkansas had sent to keep the nine students out.

The event got a lot of attention in the media. The group became known as the Little Rock Nine. The teens stayed away from the school for a few weeks. The school was finally integrated on September 25. US soldiers escorted the Little Rock Nine to the front door of the school.

FURTHER EVIDENCE

Chapter Two introduced some of the history of racial inequality in the United States. What was the main point of this chapter? What evidence is included to support this point? Go to the website below and explore information about Jim Crow laws. Find a quote that supports the chapter's main point. Does the quote support existing evidence in the chapter or add new evidence?

PBS: AMERICAN EXPERIENCE

abdocorelibrary.com/civil-rights-sit-ins

THE SIT-IN MOVEMENT BEGINS

Protesting by sitting down was not new. The Greensboro Four had been inspired by a peaceful activist named Mohandas Gandhi. Gandhi was an Indian leader known for protesting without violence. Gandhi was born in India in 1869. After studying in England, he moved to South Africa to work as a lawyer. White people ruled South Africa. They discriminated against all nonwhite people. During a train ride, railroad workers made Gandhi leave the train. He had purchased a first-class ticket. But he was

Mohandas Gandhi also faced discrimination at hotels. Those for Europeans only refused to rent him a room.

CIVIL DISOBEDIENCE

While Gandhi was jailed in South Africa, he read the essay "Civil Disobedience." Henry David Thoreau wrote the essay after going to jail for not paying his taxes. He stopped paying taxes to protest slavery. Thoreau wrote that people should protest unjust laws by breaking them. He believed people should even go to jail for their cause. He wrote, "Under a government which imprisons any unjustly, the true place for a just man is also a prison." Gandhi liked the idea of civil disobedience. He called it *satyagraha*. This Sanskrit word means "devotion to truth."

supposed to ride in third class because he wasn't white. He refused to move. Gandhi spent the next 20 years fighting racism in South Africa. He went to jail several times. He disobeyed laws he believed were unjust.

Gandhi returned to India in 1914. He thought his homeland suffered from three problems. One was British rule. Another was religious fighting. And discrimination against the lowest class was a third. Gandhi protested nonviolently. He disobeyed rules and went to jail. He and others held strikes and marches. He went on hunger strikes and refused to eat. Many Indians admired Gandhi. People around the world did too.

A COFFEE SHOP SIT-IN

In 1942, a group of college students at the University of Chicago created the Congress of Racial Equality (CORE). The students represented different races. They wanted to peacefully improve race relations in the United States. James Farmer, an African American, was one of the founders.

AUTOMOTIVE WORKERS' STRIKE, 1936–1937

In late 1936, workers at several General Motors (GM) automotive plants sat down on the job and refused to work. The largest group was at a plant in Flint, Michigan. The workers had several demands, including a better minimum wage. GM got a court order saying the workers had to leave. They stayed. GM turned off the heat. They stayed. The situation became violent when police tried to keep food from the workers. Still the workers stayed. Their sit-in stopped car production almost completely. The strike lasted 44 days. It led to a 5 percent increase in pay.

In 1942, CORE held a sit-in at a coffee shop in Chicago, Illinois. It began when James Farmer went to the coffee shop. He saw that the white worker at the coffee shop would make African-American customers wait to be served. The worker also made African Americans pay one dollar for a doughnut, while white customers only paid five cents.

Farmer had learned about Gandhi in college. Farmer wanted to try Gandhi's methods. He and other CORE members held a sit-in at the coffee shop. The manager called the police, but they did nothing. The protesters were only sitting. Finally workers served the protesters. The protesters visited the shop a few more times. They showed the business they would not tolerate racism. Other sit-ins followed. None were mass movements. But they did lead to the Greensboro sit-in.

James Farmer went on to help organize the civil rights Freedom Rides.

THE MOVEMENT GROWS

The Greensboro sit-in that began on February 1, 1960, launched a movement. Many college students were inspired by the Greensboro Four. By the end of February, students across the South held similar lunch-counter protests. In eight weeks, protesters held sit-ins in more than 70 cities.

The protests got in the way of conducting business. Protesters would sit at lunch counters. Paying customers couldn't sit and

Many students held a sit-in in Charlotte, North Carolina, on February 9, 1960.

HISTORICALLY BLACK COLLEGES AND UNIVERSITIES

Historically black colleges and universities (HBCUs) played an important role in the civil rights movement. Some hosted activities. Others were the schools many protesters attended. HBCUs are schools that were created before 1964 and that focused initially and continue to focus on educating African Americans. HBCUs also have students who aren't African American. In 2014, more than 294,000 students attended HBCUs. Nearly four-fifths were black. There are 100 HBCUs in the United States. The oldest is Cheyney University of Pennsylvania. It was founded in 1837 near Philadelphia.

have a meal. No seats were available. That kept the lunch counter from making money because of their segregation rules. These peaceful protests won over some Americans in different ways. The protests showed that African Americans found segregation unacceptable. By using nonviolence, the protesters proved themselves thoughtful and composed. This helped the

US SIT-INS

The Greensboro sit-in launched the sit-in movement. This map shows some of the cities where students held sit-ins in the first few months after Greensboro. What do you notice about the geographic locations?

harshness of segregation stand out when racists attacked protesters.

ORGANIZATIONS GET INVOLVED

Civil rights organizations also got involved in the sit-in movement. CORE was one. The Southern Christian

Leadership Conference (SCLC) was another. CORE and the SCLC taught protesters how to protest peacefully. The sit-in protesters had to remain peaceful. Nonviolence was important to the movement. It would show determination and strength.

STUDENT LEADERSHIP CONFERENCE

The sit-in movement led to a three-day meeting in April 1960. It was a student leadership conference in Raleigh, North Carolina, at Shaw University. Students talked about what happened at their sit-ins. They also planned future protests.

Ella Baker arranged the event. She was a leader of the SCLC. Baker gave a speech at the beginning of the conference. She encouraged participants to work for greater change than desegregated lunch counters. Martin Luther King Jr. backed her ideas. At the end of the conference, participants founded a new group. It was the Student Nonviolent Coordinating Committee (SNCC).

The Friendship Nine held their sit-in at McCrory's.

JAIL, NO BAIL

On January 31, 1961, nine African-American men held a sit-in at a lunch counter in Rock Hill, South Carolina. Eight of the protesters were students at Friendship Junior College. The school was close to Rock Hill. The ninth protester was a member of CORE. The group became known as the Friendship Nine.

Police arrested the nine young men. A judge gave each of them two options. They could pay a $100 fine or

RIGHTING HISTORY

In January 2015, the Friendship Nine were in court again. It was almost 54 years to the day of their sit-in and arrest in South Carolina. They were having a retrial. The judge vacated the sentence. His ruling made it as though the first trial and verdict never happened. The judge was the nephew of the original judge. He said when he cleared the original ruling, "We cannot rewrite history, but we can right history." Clarence Graham, one of the Friendship Nine, said of the ruling, "My heart was leaping. I can hold my head a little bit higher."

spend 30 days working on a chain gang. They chose the chain gang. It was a new strategy called "jail, no bail." The students didn't want to break the law and then pay money that would go toward the racist system of government. The young men did their time. They protested on the chain gang by singing. A year after the Greensboro Four protested at Woolworth, the sit-in movement was going strong. The civil rights movement had gone national.

STRAIGHT TO THE
SOURCE

On April 17, 2010, Eric Holder spoke at a celebration of SNCC's 50th anniversary. Holder was the first African-American US attorney general. He spoke about civil rights:

> *We have made tremendous progress as a nation. But it will take more than the election of the first African-American President to fully secure the promise of equality for every American. And it will certainly take more than the appointment of the first African-American Attorney General to ensure that the American justice system reflects the values and principles enshrined in our nation's founding documents.*

> Source: Eric Holder. "Attorney General Eric Holder Addresses the Student Nonviolent Coordinating Committee 50th Anniversary Conference." *Office of Public Affairs*. US Department of Justice, April 17, 2010. Web. Accessed June 12, 2017.

Consider Your Audience

Adapt this passage for a different audience, such as your family or friends. Write a blog post conveying this same information for the new audience. How does your post differ from the original text, and why?

BEYOND SIT-INS

n 1961 nonviolent protests began focusing on desegregating buses that traveled across state lines. Segregation on these buses was illegal. But many states ignored the law. CORE organized bus trips into the Deep South. These were called Freedom Rides. African-American and white protesters refused to segregate on buses. Some faced bombings and beatings. Many were arrested.

On May 29, President John F. Kennedy stepped in. He told the Interstate Commerce Commission (ICC) to integrate all the public places it managed. The ICC finally made

Some white people blocked buses filled with Freedom Riders to keep them from leaving.

35

segregation unlawful for interstate travel on November 1.

BIRMINGHAM, 1963

In 1963 civil rights leaders decided to protest in Birmingham, Alabama. The city had a reputation for being racist. Martin Luther King Jr. and other civil rights leaders planned several nonviolent protests in the city. Protests began in April.

A judge had ruled that protesting was against the law. King and others were sent to jail. They realized they would not make much progress. They needed to shock the nation.

The Children's Crusade began on May 2. Thousands of Birmingham children walked out of school. They had learned how to protest peacefully. They were going to march against segregation. Police officers with dogs confronted the children. Police officers attacked the kids with batons and water hoses. Police also arrested hundreds of the child protesters. The protests continued until May 5. The media

BLACK PANTHER BREAKFAST PROGRAM

The Black Panther Party (BPP) also fought for civil rights in the 1960s. The BPP believed in self-defense. Members often carried guns. But this image doesn't reflect the group's focus on supporting black communities. The BPP helped create schools and medical clinics. Free Breakfast for Children was one of its top programs. It gave food to kids across the nation. Melvin Dickson ran the program. He noted that the BPP showed the government's lack of work on issues such as poverty. He said, "[The US government] have all this money, but here we are, a grassroots organization feeding kids all across the US."

Children faced being sprayed with high-pressure fire hoses during the Children's Crusade.

coverage helped the cause of civil rights. People across the country saw images of the attacks in the news. Many were outraged. A few days later, city officials agreed to let the children out of jail. They also agreed to end segregation in businesses.

CIVIL RIGHTS LAWS

The civil rights movement led to new federal laws in the 1960s. The Civil Rights Act of 1964 made segregation

illegal. It also made it unlawful for companies to discriminate against a person because of his or her race, color, religion, sex, or national origin.

The Voting Rights Act of 1965 was another important civil rights law. The 15th and 19th Amendments had long ago given African-American men and women the right to vote. But some states used different methods to keep African Americans

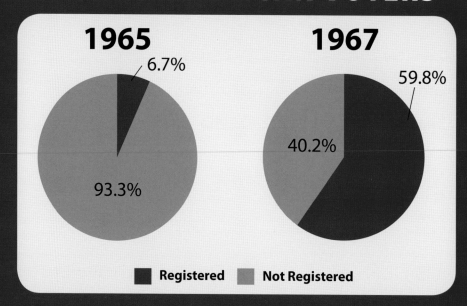

AFRICAN-AMERICAN VOTERS

1965

6.7%

93.3%

1967

59.8%

40.2%

■ Registered   ■ Not Registered

These pie charts show the percentage of African Americans registered to vote and those not registered to vote in Mississippi in 1965 and 1967. Compare the charts. What do you notice? What do you think caused the differences in the registered voters between the two years?

from voting. Some required black voters to pay a special tax. Some required them to pass a reading test. The Voting Rights Act made such practices illegal.

SIMPLE BUT POWERFUL

The Greensboro sit-in launched a movement that fueled the fight for civil rights. It was a model for peaceful protest that thousands of other Americans soon followed. Their efforts are still inspiring a new generation of activists. In the 2010s, the Black Lives Matter movement emerged to challenge the inequality African Americans still face in the United States. The movement has adopted a version of sit-ins called die-ins. Protesters lie in public places to symbolize African Americans killed by police officers.

Sitting may seem simple, but when people took a seat for civil rights, it made a difference. It told the world that people would no longer tolerate injustices. And it led to great change in the people of the United States.

EXPLORE ONLINE

Chapter Five discusses children protesting nonviolently in Birmingham in 1963. Go to the website listed below to read more about the Children's Crusade. What new information did you learn from the article? What information is similar to Chapter Five?

KING ENCYCLOPEDIA: CHILDREN'S CRUSADE

abdocorelibrary.com/civil-rights-sit-ins

FAST FACTS

- Civil rights activists used sit-ins to protest segregation in the South. They wanted to draw attention to the unfair treatment white people forced on African Americans. They also wanted to desegregate the country.

- Key players include David Richmond, Franklin McCain, Ezell Blair Jr., Joseph McNeil, Ella Baker, Martin Luther King Jr., CORE, and SCLC.

- Individual businesses became desegregated after local sit-ins.

- Sit-ins inspired people around the country to get involved in the civil rights movement.

- The movement eventually led to the Civil Rights Act of 1964, which made segregation illegal, and the Voting Rights Act of 1965, which banned tests and other methods that had been used to prevent African Americans from voting in elections.

- Sit-ins inspired the modern Black Lives Matter movement, which pushes for equality and uses similar techniques such as die-ins.

IMPORTANT
DATES

Late 1800s–early 1900s
Mohandas Gandhi models nonviolent protesting.

1957
The Little Rock Nine integrate Little Rock Central High School in Arkansas.

1960
The Greensboro Four launch a sit-in movement on February 1. In the eight weeks following the Greensboro sit-in, protesters hold sit-ins in more than 70 cities.

1961
The Friendship Nine are arrested on January 31. Civil rights activists take part in Freedom Rides.

1963
The Children's Crusade lasts from May 2 to 5.

1964
The Civil Rights Act of 1964 passes.

1965
The Voting Rights Act of 1965 passes.

STOP AND
THINK

Tell the Tale

Chapter One of this book discusses the lunch counter sit-in in Greensboro, North Carolina. Imagine you are taking part in a similar sit-in. Write 200 words about the people you encounter. What could you do to remain calm and nonviolent if someone attacks you verbally or physically?

Surprise Me

Chapter Two discusses some of the United States' history of discrimination against African Americans. After reading this book, what two or three facts about this history did you find most surprising? Write a few sentences about each fact. Why did you find each fact surprising?

Dig Deeper

After reading this book, what questions do you still have about civil rights sit-ins? With an adult's help, find a few reliable sources that can help you answer your questions. Write a paragraph about what you learned.

GLOSSARY

chain gang
a group of prisoners that work outside while chained together

desegregate
to stop separating people based on race

discriminate
to treat someone differently based on traits such as race

integrate
to stop segregating and to bring together

racism
to treat or think of someone poorly or unfairly because of his or her race

segregate
to keep groups of people apart or separated because they are of different races

sit-in
a protest in which people sit and refuse to leave

strike
a type of protest by workers in which they stop working

theology
the study of religion

ONLINE
RESOURCES

To learn more about civil rights sit-ins, visit our free resource websites below.

Visit **abdocorelibrary.com** for free Common Core resources for teachers and students, including vetted activities, multimedia, and booklinks, for deeper subject comprehension.

Visit **abdobooklinks.com** for free additional online weblinks for further learning. These links are routinely monitored and updated to provide the most current information available.

LEARN
MORE

Donohue, Moira Rose. *The Civil Rights Movement through the Eyes of Lyndon B. Johnson.* Minneapolis, MN: Abdo Publishing, 2016.

Pinkney, Andrea Davis. *Sit-in: How Four Friends Stood Up by Sitting Down.* New York: Little, Brown and Company, 2010.

ABOUT THE
AUTHOR

Duchess Harris, JD, PhD

Professor Harris is the chair of the American Studies Department at Macalester College. The author and coauthor of four books (*Hidden Human Computers: The Black Women of NASA* and *Black Lives Matter* with Sue Bradford Edwards, *Racially Writing the Republic: Racists, Race Rebels, and Transformations of American Identity* with Bruce Baum, and *Black Feminist Politics from Kennedy to Clinton/Obama*), she has been an associate editor for *Litigation News*, the American Bar Association Section's quarterly flagship publication, and was the first editor-in-chief of *Law Raza Journal*, an interactive online race and the law journal for William Mitchell College of Law.

She has earned a PhD in American Studies from the University of Minnesota and a Juris Doctorate from William Mitchell College of Law.

INDEX